Popular
Lies*
About
Graphic
Design

Published by
Actar
Barcelona / New York
info@actar.com
www.actar.com

Distribution
ActarD
www.actar-d.com

Roca i Batlle 2
E-08023 Barcelona
T +34 93 417 49 93
F +34 93 418 67 07
salesbarcelona@actar.com

151 Grand Street, 5th floor
New York, NY 10013, USA
T +1 212 966 2207
F +1 212 966 2214
salesnewyork@actar.com

First edition 2012, Barcelona
© of the edition, Actar Publishers
© of the text, Craig Ward
All Rights Reserved

ISBN 978-84-15391-35-7
DL: B- 22255-2012

Typeset in Adobe Garamond Pro
and Futura Medium.

For Lisa & Mister x

With sincere thanks to David Carson, Deanne Cheuk, Graham Clifford, Keetra Dean Dixon, Leo Jung, Christoph Niemann, Craig Redman, Chris Rubino, Michael C. Place, Stefan Sagmeister, Paul Sahre, Si Scott, James Victore, Willy Wong and Ian Wright for their respective contributions.

Further thanks to Stuart Royall.

"Popular
the greatest lie

opinion is
in the world..."

Thomas Carlyle

About This Book

This is not a book full of facts. Nor is it a book full of advice. It's a book full of opinions, and confusion between those three is how a lot of these problems begin.

Design is an undeniably broad and—crucially—non-denominational church; attracting all flavours of creative minds. There are the purists, the minimalists (and by contrast the maximalists), the avant-garde, the punks and the fetishists (more on those later); all of whom congregate in offices and studios the world over to create the great visual melting pot that is the Graphic Design landscape. Together, we create everything from corporate annual reviews to skateboard decks.

By its very nature, design caters to all manner of tastes, and this breadth of style and content ensures that, for the most part, it remains entirely subjective. It inspires everything from lively, informed debate to hate-filled, emotionally charged blog posts accompanied by reams of comments defaming this logo or that typeface.

One designer's grid is another's skulls and spray-paint and, ultimately, you're going to find your own way through it.

There are, however, a few pearls of wisdom that one hears from time to time that somehow gain groundswell. Until graphic designers from every walk of life repeat them without even thinking about what they're saying. This is design as a religion: blind adherence to a mind set or school of thought without ever questioning it. It's something to belong to, which can be appealing, particularly as so many design practitioners are self employed or studios of one. Unfortunately, a lot like religion, many of these mantras and maxims tend to be misconceptions, half truths and, in some cases, outright lies.

The aim of this book is simply an attempt to debunk these topics, clarify where appropriate and to give an opposing point of view. Not simply to be contrary (as fun as that can be), but more to consider the other side of the coin. This is more like design as science—examining other possibilities when it may be easier to side with something tried and tested. I hope you find it to be a worthwhile read.

CW

The Lies

Graphic Design is a Proper Job. 18

Comic Sans is the worst typeface ever created. 22

An education in design is pointless. 26

Having a fetish for design makes me a good designer. 32

Designers are famous. 36

Not paying for typefaces is fine. 38

Helvetica is neutral. 42

Red means hot, blue means cold. 44

USING ALL CAPITALS MEANS I'M SHOUTING. 46

A good idea doesn't require a budget. 48

The client is a $%&* 50

The client is always right. 54

Graphic Design is easy. 58

Charity clients will let you do as you please. 62

Center pages - What's the biggest lie 64
you've ever been told about design?

82   Legibility and readability are basically the same

84   Apple have good graphic design

86   Stock is a cheap solution.

90   People will want to buy my t-shirts and pin badges.

92   The rules are there to be broken.

96   Longer deadlines lead to better work.

100 The bigger, better known studios do the best work.

102 The best work wins the awards.

106 There's no budget but it's a great opportunity.

110 You've gotta get to New York.

114 Pitches are won by working late.

118 Don't have a style / You need a style.

120 Symmetry is bad.

122 You only need to use five typefaces in your career.

126 It's an urgent brief

128 Open plan offices = collaboration and better work.

132 All you need is an idea.

136 Nothing is original anymore.

140 People care about design.

144 Print is dead.

150 Postscript.

154 About the author.

"Ложь рассказ
часто станов

ал достаточно
ится истина."*

Vladimir Lenin

*"A lie told often enough
becomes the truth."

Graphic Design is a ~~Proper~~ Job

While you may protest otherwise to family members and those not in the industry, it's a harsh pill to swallow. But we should get this out of the way early on so as to better establish our stage.

Here's the thing about jobs as the vast majority of working people understand them. Monday morning rolls around. You get up, you go to your place of work and complete tasks for a set amount of hours— usually in the region of eight hours a day / forty hours a week—and on Friday afternoons you go home and forget all about it. In exchange, you are given a pre-negotiated salary paid in regular (usually monthly or similar) increments. If at any point you are required to work late, it's usually a given that you will be awarded more money as recompense in the form of overtime—usually to the tune of 1.5 to 2 times your usual hourly rate. It's a system that has worked very well for a lot of people for a long time. Roughly 99% of the population since the industrial revolution.

As a designer, you choose to step outside of this well trodden model. You will not have the luxury of set hours. Guideline hours yes, but set hours? Please! You won't even have the luxury of weekends, some of the time.

And the very second you sign the page that comes with your shiny new contract saying how you 'waive the right to overtime' and are happy to 'work whatever hours are required of you in order to complete a project,' that scratch of pen on paper is the sound of you admitting that you don't have a proper job. If you go freelance, it gets even worse as you're not even guaranteed to get paid at all; but that's another story.

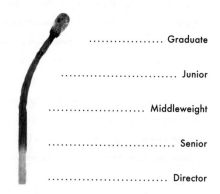

.... Graduate

.... Junior

.... Middleweight

.... Senior

.... Director

It's not a situation one can nurture for long and ultimately is something that, as you grow older, will becomes less and less appealing—that is, if you don't burn out first. Design is a young person's industry, by and large. That's not to say it favours the young as such, or that younger people are any better equipped to complete the tasks required of them; it's simply an industry that is happy to mine their enthusiasm and energy. And with some 10,000[1] students a year (in the UK alone) leaving colleges and universities with qualifications in design, it's not exactly a natural resource that is in short supply either. As for the older practitioners, they tend to remove themselves from this equation or move into more managerial roles that don't require this same commitment of hours or constant creative input and screen time.

Graphic Design is not a proper job. Being a front-line, down in the trenches designer is a lifestyle choice, and one that you can probably hang onto for about twenty years at most. So make the most of it.

* * * * *

[1] *The exact number of graduates in Graphic Design is unclear but 176,700 students graduated from Creative Arts and Design based courses in 2011. Source hesa.ac.uk*

Comic Sans

is the

worst

typeface

ever

created

Possibly the most uttered phrase in the history of design. I didn't even want to mention it but this is something I hear so often that I simply couldn't ignore it. A statement that has become popularised by design pond skimmers trying to look smart to the point that, even those with no connection to the industry of design whatsoever, know this to be a fact.

Except, it's just not true at all.

Comic Sans is a typeface that has inspired a hatred. An actual, palpable hatred. There are websites, Facebook groups and online petitions dedicated to the removal of it from society, and a variety of slogan emblazoned t-shirts, mugs, mouse mats and bumper stickers that are greedily consumed by the masses. It even made its way into an omnibus ban bill put forward by the *Ontario Model Youth Parliament* in 2005.

To be clear, this is a typeface we're talking about. A digital file. Not a murderer or some carcinogenic substance. And what's worse, it is a completely unjustified vilification. From the vitriol you read online you would be right in assuming this typeface offends designers more than any image of Third World poverty ever could.

Comic Sans is the typographic equivalent of the innocent man on death row.

It is, without doubt, an easy font to dislike. It is technically inconsistent—granted—but even the most cursory glance through any of those free typeface websites that are so prevalent will bring up all manner of terrible handwriting fonts, distressed, faux-letterpress fonts with texture already in them and weird, badly drawn copies of existing typefaces without any attention paid to the kerning and metrics, etc. Comic Sans is simply an (admittedly ugly) victim of overuse and, by virtue of that fact, misuse.

It was designed—yes, really—by *Vincent Connare*. Connare was a designer working for *Microsoft* (so, yes, perhaps another reason to dislike it for some) and it was released in 1994 after originally being created for use in *Microsoft Bob* (the argument builds). It was modelled on the hand drawn type popularised by American comic books and it was drawn, redrawn, vectored, spaced, and given time, care and attention.

It is juvenile; but for a reason. And the fact that you don't like the look of it doesn't make it the worst typeface ever.

I could point to hundreds, if not a thousand, fonts available for free from these popular websites that have had a fraction of the development time spent on them that Comic Sans enjoyed. For a typeface to be subject to national, international and ultimately global (perhaps even universal) hatred has always struck me as being very odd, and a perfect example of a self-perpetuating, quasi-religious statement about design that people cotton onto and repeat without thinking.

Back in your box, zealots.

An education in design is pointless

As college and university fees continue to rise, this is something I hear more and more and am often asked to comment on for students' dissertations and magazine articles. This, coupled with the ease of availability of design tools in the home, has led to a rise in the self-taught designer.

"Democracy..." said *Plato* '*...is a charming form of government, full of variety and disorder; and dispensing a sort of equality to equals and unequals alike.*' Democracy in design arrived in the form of desktop publishing in the 80's and now, for a couple of thousand pounds, you can kit yourself out with a reasonably comprehensive mobile design studio.

It's a subject I oscillate on. The beauty of democracy is that it's a model that permits criticism and, while educated, gainfully employed designers are perfectly capable of creating something hideous in the name of design, there is a contingent of the community that believes the reason there's so much 'ugly' design in the world comes down to the fact that anybody with access to a computer and desktop publishing software assumes they can create a flyer, a sign or whatever.

The point of this book is to be objective, so let me say this: just because I can draw a house, it does not make me an architect.

One cannot simply announce oneself as an architect. Being taught how to draw a house; learning about space, studying light, social needs, load-bearing structures, materials, energy efficiency, texture, rhythm of line and form... These things make you an architect, and it's much the same with design. Yet somehow not...

It's true that you can learn a lot from on the job experience and reading the right books. In fact, I think I learnt more in my first six months in industry than I did in the previous three years at university—mostly about reality and expectations from industry it has to be said. And I agree, that a formal education is NOT necessary for those gifted few with a natural ability to lay out information well. Those rare prodigies that are born with a knowledge of grid systems, visual hierarchy, kerning and leading type, appropriate font selection and the history of the Design practice. I'm not even being facetious; they're out there and I've met them. In fact I've met 15 year-olds who know more about design than I did at 22. The poster boy for most arguments regarding the pointlessness of design education is *David Carson*—of whom I am a huge fan. A self taught designer who went onto define a decade's aesthetic. Only, that was twenty years ago, and begs the question, how many David Carson's have there been since David Carson?

There are those that say a qualification in design doesn't guarantee you anything, and that much is true, but an education in any field counts for something and to dismiss it entirely is insulting to those who choose to study and to those who have studied before them. Likely, your future employers. For my part, I took a one year foundation course and went on to university to study design at degree level over the course of the next three years and would recommend it to anyone—not least for social reasons.

I went to university as green as they come. And yes, I emerged broke—seriously, bailiff-provokingly broke. This was in spite of my working the entire four years that I studied (a video store clerk, a bartender, a store assistant at *Staples* and finally—and weirdly—a security guard if you're interested). But the time I spent focusing on that one discipline was invaluable. I learnt about my personal strengths, my weaknesses and made friends and contacts in the industry that I was about to emerge into. I gained my Honours by writing a 17,000 word thesis that gave me a legitimate reason to study an area of the field in real depth and to contact and meet with people whose work I admired and whose opinions I respected. I learnt new techniques, about former practitioners, new ways of thinking and of approaching problems. I tried working with letterpress for the first time and learnt how to screenprint and etch. I learnt about colour theory, typography, deadlines and how to critique my own work and that of other people. I attended lectures by those in industry and, damn it, I even met my future wife at university. I was lucky enough to have a couple of great and inspirational tutors along the way—not all of them I hasten to add—and I found work after a short internship arranged through my university.

With that said, a degree does not guarantee you a job when you do finally graduate, but nor should it—you still need to show good work at the end of it. The degree or qualification is for the love of it. It shows a willingness to learn, to struggle, a commitment to the industry and a belief in the importance of process and in the passing on of knowledge.

An education in design is not always necessary, I agree, but it is most definitely not pointless.

Having a
fetish for design
makes me a
good designer

Congratulations! You have an exceptionally well observed graphic design blog—maybe even several —that are updated multiple times a week. You have a heaving and yet carefully curated collection of other people's work on your *Tumblr* page and a blossoming *Twitter* account with several hundred followers who lap up your opinions. You *Digg* stuff regularly, you were amongst the first few hundred on *Ffffound*. You 'Like' groups like 'Typography is Hot' on *Facebook* and you're fully *LinkedIn* with over 600 connections in industry, (90% of whom you've never even met). Your formidable *Flickr* stream is kept up to the moment, you're *Pinterest*-ed in everything from interiors to Swiss poster design and you listen to every design related podcast going. Your bookshelf sags in the middle from weighty, authoritative graphic design tomes, you have a collection of beautifully crafted vinyl toys from *Kid Robot*, a wardrobe swollen with graphic print t-shirts, an enviable selection of scanned vintage type samples from the 1800's and you attend design related talks, seminars, mornings and festivals the world over.

And not one of these things makes you a better designer. Do some work.

The internet has changed the way we interact with and consume design in many ways and, over the last few years, has brought with it a new breed of people with a keen interest in—nay, a fetish for—design. People who really, *really* love design and yet, are essentially incapable of creating anything themselves, so mired are they in consuming other people's work

and opinions. They talk about it, blog about it and engage with it in all of the ways I mentioned above, but the one thing they forget to do is to actually find time to be a designer. Pointing no fingers, there are hubs for design that perpetuate this. Former design studios that now do nothing more than curate their blogs showing other people's work and sell ad space to make a living. It all feels very strange to me.

Perhaps it's a sign of the times. Perhaps there's just not enough work to go around. But there are now so many ways to procrastinate in the name of design—particularly online—that it amazes me how anything gets done at all anymore. The community of design is important—exceptionally so—and it's a fact that nepotism will get you further in life than any amount of talent, so I'm certainly not about to deny the importance of remaining connected to the industry at large. Maintaining your online presence is vital today, but not a week goes by without me getting invited to another portfolio hosting site or an offer of 'connecting with others' in some new, previously unforeseen way, and this expectation that every designer keeps up with every form of online media is simply unsustainable; the whole arena is completely over-saturated.

Just remember, at the end of the day, no designer ever got hired for a job because they had a good *Tumblr* stream. Or not to my knowledge at least.

I'm serious. Jump in. Do some work.

Designers
are
famous

Everything in life is relative. Even those precious few designers considered '*rock stars*' within the industry would have difficulty getting arrested.

I used to live on the same block as *Stefan Sagmeister*'s studio in New York and would see him a couple of mornings a week. Mr. Sagmeister—an immensely talented and industry savvy individual—is probably about as famous as a Graphic Designer can get, but I can confirm there were no screaming groupies stopping him from getting through the door. No paparazzi hounding him to his waiting car. In fact, no car either for that matter. The idea of designer as celebrity simply doesn't exist. Even the talking head designers that get asked to comment in the mainstream press are only usually wheeled out to defend or discuss the occasional design atrocity that has the public in uproar—see, for example the *London Olympics logo* or *New York City*'s most recent rebranding, etc.

You may, if you're lucky, get to work on some high profile work over the course of your career, and your name may even make the credits of a TV show, book jacket or album cover; but essentially your awards, portfolio and t-shirts will mean nothing to the general public. The important thing, you'll come to realise, is that you make work that you can be proud of and look back on fondly.

Not paying for typefaces is fine

No, it's theft. And outside of the obvious moral issues here there are other reasons, but first, a confession.

I stole the font library from my first job—working as a Junior Designer at an advertising agency in London. The entire thing I just dumped off the server and copied onto a CD the day before I left. Some 20,000 typefaces from the *Adobe* collections, *Linotype*, *Red Rooster*, *Identikal*, and myriad others. I was quite pleased with myself at the time, and enjoyed browsing the collection, making sheets of print outs and binding them together in little books... See the section on '*Having a fetish for Design*' (page 32). Not cool.

19,984 of those typefaces I never touched. It was simply an overwhelming amount. And the ones that I did use were often used gratuitously and for the sake of it.

I threw away the CD a few years ago after I found it collecting dust in a broken case.

While I could never subscribe *Massimo Vignelli*'s assertion that you should only use five typefaces in your whole career (page 122), our point is the same. You should build your own font library. There are basic styles that you should tick off, but try to give it a personality and an opinion. Buy the fonts you really, genuinely like enough to be willing to pay for. Respect them; treat them as tools for communication—which is exactly what they are. Don't try and rationalise not paying for fonts because they're expensive; they're not. A hairdresser's scissors can cost a fortune, for example. A good typeface will have had months of work put into it and for a typographer to make any money at all, he would need to sell a lot of copies of their font. You get to pay for it just once—maybe less than fifty pounds—and keep and use these fonts for the rest of your life. They won't go blunt, or break and you may use them a thousand times or only a handful.

The point is, if you have too many fonts and you haven't paid for them, there can be a tendency to disrespect them, to treat them as disposable items and make bad decisions regarding their use. Less, in this instance, is most definitely more.

Helvetica

is

neutral

Often mistaken as being vanilla, Helvetica is really anything but neutral. It has permeated society like virtually no other font and is essentially as ubiquitous a typeface as has ever existed. That much is true. But this ubiquity mustn't be confused with neutrality. Through its usage in so many pieces of signage and official communications—particularly in the USA—it has become something else altogether. A direct and authoritative typeface with a very distinct tone of voice, far removed from its original intended use.

Look harder if you're actually trying to be neutral (and moreover, ask yourself why that is the case). The right font is out there, but bear in mind that very few communications should actually be aimed at no-one in particular.

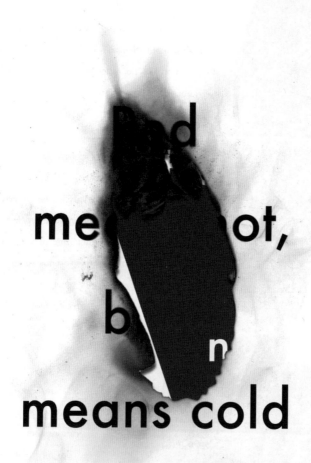

Red means hot,
b n means cold

Half-arsed and over-used semiotics like these are rife in communications of all kinds. Green means natural or organic. Pink is feminine... It goes on. The advertising industry has to be the very worst at this, often due in part to a box-ticking, uneducated client or a lack of imagination from all parties involved.

You're never more aware of how pedestrian designers and clients can be when standing in the supermarket staring at, say, air fresheners or toothpaste packaging. It's the most frustrating thing to see every product with a certain demographic looking virtually identical.

We're constantly told that consumers like choices; so why not give them something to choose from?

There is always another way to communicate what you need to without resorting to trite assumptions like these, and it's the designer's role—nay, prerogative— to come up with new ways of communicating often well-trodden information in new, yet relevant ways.

USING ALL CAPITALS MEANS I'M SHOUTING

As with the last example, there are so many typographic old-wives tales out there that it was tough to know which one to pick. *Italics infer speed*, for example.

Your primary font selection and those you combine it with, the manner in which you lay out the typography and the colour selection will convey your tone of voice much more effectively. Whether you should use all capitals or not is another question entirely and should be treated on a case by case basis. A lot of my work has successfully used all caps and rarely have I been shouting.

Bear in mind, setting a six word headline in caps is one thing, setting an entire passage of text in capitals is another.

A good idea doesn't require a budget

I'm hard pushed to call this a lie as its heart is definitely in the right place, but it's also a very naïve statement and glosses over a lot of factors. If you have an idea that pivots on a single, highly expensive realisation that can be achieved in no other way then, in all likelihood, it's probably not a very good idea. But equally, if you have a thought that by extension happens to require some more expensive equipment to create then that shouldn't detract from the quality of the idea itself.

I've managed to cajole many people into working with me on a shoestring—which is something I actually hate doing, as I think talented people should get paid properly—but ultimately, corners get cut and the final piece can end up feeling or looking compromised if you're not careful. Sometimes you just need to spend some money. And if you don't have the money, you need to get inventive very quickly and be extremely nice to people.

At that point, the enthusiasm of others for the project will act as a very effective barometer for whether it's a good idea or not.

The

client

is a

$%&*

The classic post-work, tie-loosening, pub-venting favourite. OK, I admit it, who hasn't unloaded on an account handler, co-worker or peer regarding the decisions and opinions of a client?

It's an easy thing to do. You've spent weeks nurturing an idea. Loving it, crafting it, honing it to the peak of perfection (in your eyes). And then comes the presentation. And immediately, something is called into question. The colour. The headline. The layout. The logo placement or size thereof. Punctuation. It can be really frustrating to take your work back to the drawing board but, here's the bad news; no agency or design firm is going to pay you to satisfy your own naval-gazing ideas or concepts—as appealing as that might seem—and no matter how much the agency you're interviewing at sells themselves on the emphasis they put on your creativity, the client comes first. And always will.

The relationship that exists between client and designer informs every piece of work you do with them—and it should be 'with' not 'for'.

The first time you work with a client you should expect to have to sell an idea in. They have no reason to trust you. There is no such thing as inherited respect and you're only as good as your last job for that particular client. They rarely care about work you've created for other brands.

Conversely, if you're several projects into a relationship and still having to convince the client of every decision you make, then you may want to re-examine the arrangement. What are you doing that makes them not trust you? How can you better explain your ideas? And ultimately, do you want to continue working with someone who doesn't trust you? It's always tough to get good work out, but that's why published work is so much more vital and telling of a designer's talents than self-initiated work. Both are important, but it's not enough to have an idea anymore, you have to get it out there. Anyone can have ideas. In fact everyone does.

Honesty throughout the entire process is key, as is keeping everyone on the same page. Turning up to present work after three weeks of radio silence never bodes well—it's important to realise that not everyone lives inside your head. If you're not confident something you're presenting will be achievable or is going to work, express your concerns as opposed to letting it fall apart half way down the line when it's already been bought into. Cost things out appropriately up front. Don't go looking for more money, don't overcharge and, if the fee is justifiably high, break it down and explain the costs.

Keeping your client up to speed throughout the design process will help them to feel included, well serviced and hopefully inspire them to come to you with more work in future. Even if they don't come back, if nothing else, they'll understand the process a little better and hopefully make their next designer's life a little easier, so maybe just do it for the karma.

The
client
vays
ght

As with the previous point, remaining honest with your client is key. The client is not always right, and if a suggestion has been made (or worse still, a drawing...) that you disagree with, plainly explain why you don't believe this to be the solution. Don't, for goodness' sake, do the amend 'just to show them' —that's something I've seen backfire a thousand times. And you know what? From time to time, your client will make a suggestion that actually benefits a project, so don't immediately go on the defensive when requests and amends come in.

It's always hard to remain objective after spending weeks or more staring at something and believing that this is the only way it can possibly exist. But it's something you have to learn to do and retaining a professional distance from projects will make your life a lot easier. The urban myth that *Peter Saville* never made a client amend in his career is exactly that, and to expect to do whatever you please on every project is professionally unworkable.

In addition; pick your battles. If the client wants to see a slightly darker red than you have used, ask yourself if this will really compromise the overall design? Conversely, if they were happy with blue throughout the entire process and have suddenly changed their mind to dark red, then by all means ask them why. Explain why you believe this will not work, the effects it will have on the project overall and, where relevant, any extra costs that will be incurred. As soon as money comes into the equation you'll be surprised by how much can be left to slide... As a rule of thumb I budget for four rounds of amends within a project. Sometimes you get it right first time, more often you don't. No matter how good you are or believe yourself to be, be ready for the latter.

Ultimately, you're being paid to provide a service and a skill. That much is important to remember and for your client to respect. But also important to remember is the fact that humans make mistakes and are equally liable to change their mind with no notice. Very few clients know what they want from the beginning of a project, so you simply have to bear with them.

▼

NewFinal_highRes_V5b_amended

Today 3:30 AM

Graphic

design

is

easy

In as much as '*Graphic Design is Not a Proper Job*' (page 18), neither is it something that could ever be called easy. If you're doing it properly, that is. Frustratingly of course, the very best practitioners, design maestros like the *Paul Rands* of the world, however, can truly make the craft appear effortless.

When a headline or piece of communication is presented in such a way that you can't imagine it ever looking any other way; when you can't pick a hole in the kerning of a single pair of letters; when you are struck between the eyes by a treatment so perfect that it seems almost familiar, and the elegant colourway and choice of typeface is pitch perfect… That is effortless design. To the casual observer, it may look like a simple task—and the tools we use are getting better and better (and making us lazier and lazier). For the rest of us, we have to work at it. We have to squint at the screen and stay up late. Walk away from it for days at a time, come back to it, start again, change things up, throw it away and try different typefaces in various combinations before finally—often begrudgingly—sending the work to print. Shaking our head as the file uploads wondering if there were something we could have done for it to be better.

Ultimately, we might never want to look at the work again, let alone see it displayed for fear of finding fault with it. Rest assured that's a feeling that never goes away, even with the maestros and is a natural feeling—this is something that is going out into the world with your name against it after all.

Something else that people often overlook is the actual physical exhaustion that can come from spending hours at your desk. Being a designer isn't the same as working on a building site or labouring at the coalface of course, but creativity in itself; thinking conceptually—let alone time spent in front of a screen—can be tiring in as much the same way as driving for long periods can. Maintaining your concentration and long-term focus on a project, often late at night and for extended periods of time, can be gruelling stuff.

Charity

clients will

let you

do a

you pl

If you find yourself hoping to net some easy awards or portfolio showpieces by working for charities at a cut price rate on the proviso that you have complete freedom, think again.

Charities work extremely hard to build up their public image. They do so with dignity and the work they do is generally selfless. As not-for-profit institutions they usually have very little or no budget so many designers approach them with the promise of great work in exchange for complete creative freedom. A skim through the awards annuals reveal a disproportionately high amount go to campaigns and projects conducted for charities. Remember though that these awards are given in spite of a lack of budget, not because of it.

If you've approached charities with this kind of offer before, you'll know that it really doesn't wash with most of them and they expect the same treatment as a full-paying clients. As they should.

And you? Well you should just be pleased with the karma. Shame on you.

What's the
biggest lie

you've ever
been told
about design?

* * * * *

Firstly, that "You can't judge a book by its cover."
If the designer has done their job, you should
absolutely be able to do this.

Also, "You have to know the rules to be able to break them". I have no
training, no schooling [in design] and I never learned all the rules. People
claim I have broken them, but whatever. It's worked out quite nicely.

David Carson

http://www.davidcarsondesign.com

Something that has driven generations of school kids crazy...

From kindergarten onwards, we always learned that yellow + red = orange (true), yellow + blue = green (true-ish), but we also learned that red + blue = purple.

And that last one is obviously a lie. Since red is of course 100% magenta and 100% yellow, when you mix it with any kind of blue it will always turn brown.

But somehow this evil lie keeps on being perpetuated, pushing scores of eager young artists to despair.

Christoph Niemann
http://www.christophniemann.com

Years ago, when I was solely a book jacket designer, I was told that "you can't use more than two typefaces on a cover."

This bad advice (read: lie) sent me in the unintended direction of using as many typefaces as I could as often as I could.

James Victore
http://www.jamesvictore.com

"They'll always choose the expected."

To expound, when a client is given a few design directions to choose from, they will lean towards the most familiar.

I typically include a some what 'safe' option—an approach I am sure will make the client smile. But the majority of my design directions are two steps beyond what I would expect anyone to say yes to. It is rare that the 'safe' contender wins. A little risk, and hopefully some forward progression, can be the main point of appeal.

Keetra Dean Dixon

http://www.fromkeetra.com

I'm not sure if this is a lie really, but this is something that was said to me—and that at the time I embraced—that I disagree with now. It was from an old professor of mine who was using this as an argument to justify the need (or maybe the future need) for the graphic designer in society. It went something like this:

"If you want proof that the Graphic Designer is needed, just take a walk down the street. Our visual world is a confusing, messy and ugly place."

At the time I remember being very empowered by this statement. I now view it as a poor justification for committing to a life as a Graphic Designer. In retrospect it seems subjective, impractical and a bit elitist. Even if you accept the idea that things are a mess, who or what is responsible? People? The lack of design?

Everything around us—with the exception of nature—is already designed by people.

So while I would admit that my role as a designer involves ordering, clarifying and sometimes even prettying-up [information], I can't image a worse situation than having designer's hold sway over every aspect of our visual world.

Beauty and order and understanding often come from mistakes, spontaneity and things unplanned.

Paul Sahre
http://www.paulsahre.com

"Computers are not where it's at, lad."
Barry Dipper, my tutor at Newcastle College.

"You will never get anywhere doing design."
Christopher Gibson Place, my Dad, God bless him.

Michael C Place
http://www.wearebuild.com

* * * * *

"Memorise the Quark Express keyboard shortcuts."

Leo Jung
http://www.leojung.com

A popular lie about graphic design:
"The computer is just a tool."

It is not. You are the tool.

Stefan Sagmeister
http://www.sagmeister.com

* * * * *

"Good design goes unnoticed"
and "Designers don't get to travel..."

Chris Rubino
http://www.chrisrubino.com

"Stay small" was a piece of advice I heard quite often when I began my career. Smaller studios and a small circle of clients—I was told—meant more control and thus [work of a] higher quality. In fact, go solo if you could.

Nowadays, I find that nothing happens in a silo and that everything is connected. If you've got sharp kerning skills, good intentions, and the ingenuity to spin gold out of thin air, why not add solid management skills to your belt and be able to kill it at scale? The world seems to need designers more than ever. What's wrong with being part of a group, playing in a team, forming a league, building a community? Not everyone has the capacity to manage process, budgets, expectations or personalities, but if you got 'em, why not go for it? Balls out!

Willy Wong
http://www.willywong.com

"Less is more!"

Milton Glaser

http://www.miltonglaser.com

"We don't have any money."

It's that whole tiresome act of the client pleading poor and screwing you down to the dollar. Then you find out later they paid a million bucks for some other component of the project...

Craig Redman
http://www.craigandkarl.com

My art teacher in 12th grade told me that Graphic Designers got to design toothpaste boxes, and that was honestly why I chose to study graphic design.

I have yet to design a toothpaste box.

Deanne Cheuk
http://www.deannecheuk.com

I was told, before I went to college that it would all be over by the time I was 40. I'm now way past that, and I've still got lots to do!

Also, on leaving college (with a very bad degree mark), the new head of the course—whom I had never met before—told me I would never be able to teach. I happily taught and ran the final year courses at Camberwell and Brighton for quite a few years.

Ian Wright
http://www.mrianwright.co.uk/

On my first day on the job of a (now defunct) ad agency in London, I was told I couldn't start any work until I had a Graphic Artists' License and I was dispatched to the local Post Office to apply. After a frustrating hour I realised I'd been had. Oh how they laughed when I got back to the agency.

On the second day I was sent out to the art store for a can of tartan paint. Lesson learned.

Graham Clifford
http://www.grahamclifforddesign.com/

"You'll never get anywhere in this
industry without kissing a lot of arse
along the way."

Si Scott
http://www.siscottstudio.com/

* * * * *

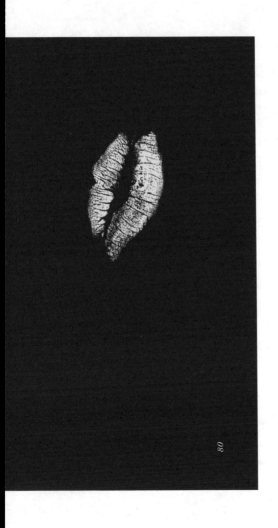

LEGIBILITY AND READABILITY ARE BASICALLY THE SAME

This is why you study. See *An Education in Design is Pointless* (pg 26). I didn't intend this to be an educational book so I won't go into it here, suffice to say there are plenty of places you can't look.

Apple

have

good

graphic

design

This statement could fuel a book all of its own. *Apple*'s design, on closer inspection, is actually all over the place in my opinion, and sits on two sides of a very defined line.

The clean lines and simple geometry of their iconic product design are all but forgotten and tossed to the kerb when sat alongside their icon, navigation and interface design where everything has a bevel, a drop shadow and a glossy 'button' effect. Their packaging design has remained unchanged in essence for a long time now and adopts a kind of utilitarian approach. A photograph of the product in profile (tick); face on (tick); on white (tick); with a reflection (tick). Fine. But inoffensive and very formulaic. All bad words, particularly for a designer working for them in-house.

What *Apple* do have is extremely good marketing, PR and mass-market appeal because of it. The flurry of imitators to adopt their design style is testament to this fact—*Apple* were the only ones to whisper in a very shouty field—but please don't, for a second, hold it up as 'good' Graphic Design. Hold it up as functional, clean and unfussy design. And then curse them for pioneering the glossy button style app icon that suddenly everyone was using. For everything.

Stock

is a

cheap

solution

OK, I get it. There isn't always a budget for photography. In fact, that's become the norm where it used to be the exception. But stock *anything* —be it photography, imagery, icons or illustration—are all very much a part of the reason for this situation in the first place.

Whether it's a selection of free ink splat *Photoshop* brushes, a cheap photograph, a vector icon or an entire website template, it will never truly marry with your original vision for the design and handing over this responsibility for a part or a whole of your design to something you haven't had complete control over will ultimately lead to a disjointed and incoherent finished piece. And it really sticks out.

I'm not being entirely naïve here; I've had to use stock images on work before, but if your work requires and is built around the use of imagery, try and have the client sign off on a photography budget early on. That should be a no-brainer and goes back to keeping clients on the same page. If it's not an option, try and consider alternative options for the design. Don't agree to provide them with images that you have taken or will take. Getting yourself into a position where you're the designer AND illustrator/photographer can be very problematic and another short cut to total burn-out.

Stock imagery has basically ruined the photography industry. I know several very talented photographers who can barely scrape a living because of it, in fact a lot of would-be career photographers need a second income to get by. And the more I see Graphic Design saturated with stock textures, logos, icons and illustrative elements I can't help but feel we'll go that way soon enough too.

The whole thing very quickly becomes bland, cheap and homogenised.

People will want to buy your pin badges and t-shirts *

*They probably won't. Sorry.

The rules

are mere

to be

broken

This loaded and over-used phrase both insinuates and assumes a lot of things; one being that design requires rules to be successful.

There are a large number of practitioners who see design as being more successful and expressive when it is loose and when rules are not adhered to. For my part (this is a book of opinions), I see it as more of a half truth, as opposed to an outright lie. Once you know what the rules are in the first place (see *'An Education in Design is Pointless'*, page 26) and you have a very good cause for breaking them, then and only then, should you consider doing something outside of 'the law'.

A disregard for accepted practices and theory can provide a very exciting, even thrilling, piece of communication, but equally, being some kind of design *enfant terrible* just for the sake of it, can often lead to a disjointed, awkward and ultimately unsatisfying portfolio or piece of work. A magazine where every page is different with no continuity in its layout may have been cutting edge once upon a time but now, with hindsight, you realise that it's just difficult/annoying to read or even illegible.

A better tactic is to be smart about it and come at things from a different angle—exploit the rules that are there. How can you make them best benefit your project? The rules of design are surprisingly forgiving. By learning them, as you evolve as a designer, a lot of minor decisions will already be subconsciously made for you. It'll still be your head making the decision but you instinctively know, for example, that you shouldn't set more than thirteen words on one line of text and you'll know why placing elements in certain places looks better than in others. As this happens, you'll find making decisions about which rules to follow comes much more easily, and the times that you find you do need to go off-piste, you'll no doubt have a very good reason to do so.

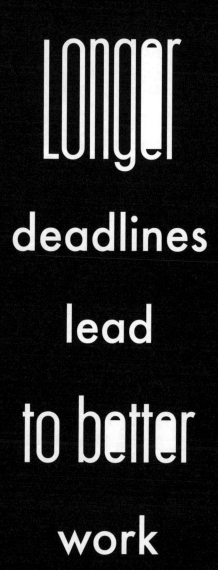

Longer

deadlines

lead

to better

work

I can only speak from personal experience, but over the course of my career I've had projects that have lasted from one hour to over a year.

Early in my career I worked for a while at a start-up agency and, as the sole designer on several projects, I was required to create look-and-feel visuals, logos, posters and concepts in a very short period of time—sometimes hours. I hated it. Why wasn't I being taken seriously? Why wasn't design being taken seriously?! How I longed for the halcyon days of university where I would have an entire term/semester to complete a project—and a project that I had conceived at that. All I wanted was a *proper* project with an appropriate amount of time allocated to research, re-research, develop, test and evolve the work. At that time, to make matters worse, I had friends working at publishers and branding agencies who would routinely spend months at a time on their logos and annual reports. How I envied them.

What this time taught me, though, was to have a belief in my early ideas and I became quite good at coming up with a couple of concepts and working them up very quickly. Going with my gut.

When I left the start-up, I went to a (supposedly) much more grown up company with much larger clients and, immediately, the gestation period for projects lengthened. Campaigns and projects would take several months as round after round went into testing, re-testing and beyond. I began to struggle and lose focus. You might call it a form of *Stockholm Syndrome* but I really missed the old days at the start up. As if this wasn't bad enough, my next job was at an even bigger agency; one of the largest in the world, in fact.

Over the course of the next two years there, I saw no more than two projects go live. Over 95% of what I produced fizzled out in boardroom purgatory and, of those two projects, just one now resides in my portfolio. Not a particularly good investment for two years of fifty or sixty hour work weeks.

My experience may be unique. But for my money, you rarely need more than a few weeks for most still image projects. Obviously, if you're attempting something more ambitious, or time related, then you may need longer but, really, three or four rounds of amends over the course of a couple of weeks is usually ample. Much more and you can end up wasting your time chasing unworkable ideas or losing focus, much less and you may feel under too much pressure to deliver and that, in itself, can be equally stifling.

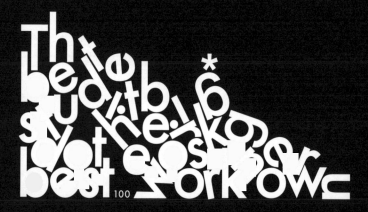

Let's not confuse *'best work'* with *'best-known work'*. To my last point, the bigger agencies may get to work with larger, more visible clients but, with those clients come more meetings, more presentations to more people and more opinions having to be taken into account on each project. Good ideas very easily get buried.

The designers and studios I come back to from time to time—those whose work I most admire—are more often than not individuals or small, dynamic teams that can operate under the radar. This also means they're often overlooked in awards shows (often because they don't enter them—another discussion entirely). Don't for one moment think a big (in name or size) employer will guarantee you better work. That responsibility remains squarely with you.

* * * * *

The best

work

wins the

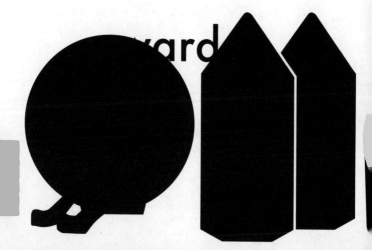

Pencils, double ended golden pencils, black monoliths, statues, arrows, certificates, brass lions, glass cubes... The creative trophy cabinet can make for a pretty ugly skyline, but these often Freudian, totemic objects are cherished by many corners of the industry.

With the odd exception, the cost of entering awards shows is forever on the increase and, having been a jury member occasionally, I can testify that the judging systems are usually less than perfect. In some of the more poorly organised schemes, work is often seen out of context (or worse, simply on screen) by people from vastly different backgrounds and with so many images and paragraphs of explanations, meanings can be easily lost in translation.

For these reasons, a lot of the smaller shops and individual practitioners choose not to put their work up for awards. Some designers even see them as pointless. While I wouldn't go that far, I can attest that if you're entering awards purely for some kind of validation then you're probably entering for the wrong reasons.

Your work needs to make you proud first and foremost and, if you find yourself in a position where you want to share this work with your peers—perhaps as a form of self-promotion—then by all means, fill out that entry form and write that cheque. But then seriously just cross your fingers, it really can be a lottery.

There's no budget, it's a great opportunity

And that would be an opportunity for what exactly?

If you go your entire career without receiving this kind of a proposition, you're doing either extremely well or extremely badly depending on your mind set. The idea that it's OK for you to spend days of your time creating work for world renowned clients who aren't paying you a decent wage is pretty shameful— yet often unavoidable. Unless you set your stall out very early on and stick to your guns.

As a designer, you want that client's brand in your portfolio and, of course, they know this.

The exception to this rule should probably be charity work, (though manage your expectations, see '*Charity clients will let you do as you please*', page 62) but my personal rule is to only accept direct approaches from charities themselves—as opposed to an award-hungry creative agency. Rest assured the Art Director commissioning you will not be giving up his/her wage to work on the project and nor should you be expected to in that case. Ten years in, I'm more confident in telling people where to go. In fact something I like to do is to ask the person emailing/calling me "Are you getting paid to ask me?" That's always a fun one.

Continually accepting these kinds of '*opportunity briefs*' will ultimately cheapen your own perception of your work and that filters through to the work itself. You can often tell when a portfolio is full of '*opportunities*', particularly when you've been working in industry for a while.

It used
to be the
case that
to go where
work was,
the

I wish I could say I had the resolv
to turn away from these ki
of propositions but I'm as
as the next designer, a
honest, some of th
have led to more w
paying clients. A
rests with you

I wish I could say I had the resolve
to turn away from these kinds
of propositions but I'm as guilty
as the next designer, and, if I'm
honest, some of those projects
have led to more work from better
paying clients. Again, the decision
rests with you.

You gotta get

It used
to be the
case that
you had to go where
the work was,
and in the
past that
meant
moving to
your nearest
large city where
commercial opportunities
for designers were more
plentiful.

to New York*

I now live in New York
and prior to that I was
based in London, but
the fact is that 99%
of my projects come
in over email (or over
the phone) from all
over the globe. I could, in fact,
work anywhere I choose
to: my geographical
location has very little to
do with my
output.

*London
Paris
Barcelona
Berlin
etc.

Designers hail from extremely diverse backgrounds and I've found that their address bears little or no relation to the quality of the content of their portfolios.

What is true, for my part, is that you're likely to find more inspiration in cities—if that's your thing. More galleries, more people, more of a network... it goes on. But then it depends on what you find inspiring. It may be that you take inspiration from nature and the great outdoors. From staring out over grassy meadows or sitting on a mountain top stargazing. What you take from your surroundings and put back into your work differs for everyone.

The bigger agencies do set up in bigger cities— but to that point, see 'The bigger, better known studios do the best work' (page 100). And here's another thing; so ingrained is this particular idea that, in the UK alone, almost half of the 10,000 graduating design students each year will flock down to London looking for work. Personally, I don't like those odds right now.

Dare to step outside of what tends to be expected; the internet has made that possible, so embrace it. Let your work do the talking, not your post code.

Pitches

are won

by

walking

It's a fact that in an agency, 80% of the actual creative work will be done in the two days before a new business pitch. The fact that the brief has been with the agency for three months, seemingly mired or lost in the planning department, is irrelevant: you're still going to have to pull a couple of all-nighters the days before the deadline.

But that's what pitches are about, right? Working late, take-away curries at 11pm, beers at the office, bags under your eyes, sleeping on the reception sofa, the camaraderie and team spirit... Please! It's more often down to an agency working everyone at 95% capacity, so when the opportunity to win new business does come in, it gets shoehorned in around existing briefs as opposed to being given the time it deserves.

This said, there are a lot of reasons why I'll never be a successful businessman.

At their best, pitches are an amazing opportunity. An unshackled chance to show what you and your agency can do. Few budget considerations. No threat of several rounds of amends. One shot. They're not supposed to be a chance to prove how late you can work, on how little sleep and how well you can push images around onscreen until they happen to fall into an arrangement that isn't entirely upsetting.

While this assumes an agency of a certain size, the best model for running a pitch, in my opinion, is to divide the time allowed thus: 35% planning and strategy, 25% brainstorming and idea generation for the execution, 35% of the time to actually create the work and allow that last 5% for your printer breaking down (it will, it always does) and production time; mounting, binding etc. If run properly, no-one needs to spend the night before the presentation at the office and turn up, bleary eyed at the train station.

A .... Planning

B .... Idea Generation

C .... Work Creation

D .... Printer breakdown buffer

Don't
have
a
styl[e]
[y]ou
need
a
style

Whichever one of these you've been told, be assured that the opposite is bound to be true. As I said in the introduction, ultimately, you're going to find your own way through your career.

My personal feeling is that (unless they're being hired for such a purpose) if a designer approaches a brief with a preconceived notion of how the final piece will appear (i.e. 'in their style') then it has already failed as a piece of communication. Projection of oneself onto a project in such a way transforms your work into more of an illustration than a piece of communication. And again, if that's the idea then fine, but for most design it's simply not appropriate.

Conversely, some of the most successful designers out there have had their styles. It makes your work recognisable and it makes you easy to deal with. Clients know what to expect; everyone knows what to expect. Great, but where's the fun in knowing essentially how something is going to look before you've even begun? There are arguments for both scenarios but the only person who needs to be happy with your portfolio is you. And hopefully your clients. Don't feel obliged to force a style onto yourself and, equally, don't chase other people's styles or zeitgeist-y looks. That, in particular, does nothing more than to age the work prematurely.

Symmetry is bad

Symmetry is only bad if one half of the symmetry is boring to begin with, plus there are various kinds of symmetry. Horizontal symmetry can be dull, yes, but radial, rotational or axial symmetries offer you a lot of options. I think every designer should explore working with symmetry, there can be something very pleasing about it. Please don't rule something out because you've heard it's bad.

Symmetry
is bad

Symmetry is only bad if one half of the symmetry is boring to begin with, plus there are various kinds of symmetry. Horizontal symmetry can be dull, yes, but radial, rotational or axial symmetries offer you a lot of options. I think every designer should explore working with symmetry, there can be something very pleasing about it. Please don't rule something out because you've heard it's bad.

You only

need five

typefaces

to last

your career

Massimo Vignelli is a very smart man. We would disagree on a lot, I have no doubt, but I have been happy to quote and paraphrase him several times throughout my career.

I even began my final year thesis with his accurate and succinct definition of Graphic Design ("...*the communication of information in an appropriate visual manner*"). This assertion, however, is one of his most-quoted: that you only need five typefaces to last you your entire career. Specifically Garamond, Bodoni, Helvetica, Univers and Century were the ones he was referring to.

A notorious hard-liner, Vignelli's point is that a designer with only a few tools to choose from will make better choices.

I have already talked about the importance of curating your type collection (page 38) and, to an extent, I agree. However my personal opinion is that placing such restrictions on yourself can be extremely limiting, creatively speaking. It's simply a case of being judicious. A builder working with only five tools will probably get by, but they will struggle when they need a different sized screwdriver.

I like to begin a project with a simple exercise that's similar to the way Vignelli suggests working; by setting the type in a serif, a sans serif, a slab serif, a script and an italic, just to see how it feels in each. That's basically all you've got to work with typographically; everything else is just a variation on each of these themes. Some will immediately feel wrong and from there you can select the style that feels right and begin to explore alternatives. The subtleties of type design mean that there is a font for every occasion and it's your task as a designer to isolate and select it.

Imagine if we all lived by the five font maxim? We'd have no *Höefler & Frere-Jones*, no *House Industries*, no *Identikal* and certainly no *Virus Fonts*. Extend it further and you could argue that there'd be no need for so many design agencies or designers. For me, that makes for a pretty bland typographic landscape. It's the diversity inherent in industry that makes it such a pleasure to be a part of.

-

Aa Bb Cc Dd Ee

It's
an
urgent
brief

When you get the call—and you will—on a Friday afternoon requiring visuals for the following Monday, all this really means is that someone, somewhere, higher up in the chain of command, has dropped the ball. A diary has been mismanaged, a meeting has been forgotten about and, consequently, a project hasn't been briefed.

There are very few genuinely urgent jobs in the world. Don't be afraid to question people when they do come in. No children will die if this flyer doesn't get printed... TONIGHT! No wars will break out if that banner ad doesn't get uploaded... IMMEDIATELY!

It's very easy to get caught up in that world, but retaining a sense of perspective is vital, lest you become consumed by it.

Open plan
offices

=

collaboration

& better work

There's a problem here, and you're made to sound like a dinosaur if you disagree with it.

At some point in the early 21st Century, virtually every agency in the world decided to tear down its walls, democratise their space and drag senior partners, kicking and screaming from their offices to sit amongst the proletariat.

Now, here we all are. In the cold light of day. Stranded in the middle of white, call centre like spaces, looking at each other. And we are ugly. We're able to see exactly who is working on what, taking lunch when, leaving at what time and talking to whom at all times.

The idea was pure and sound: without walls we will collaborate more. We will talk to people that we didn't before and we will share our ideas and thoughts. A creative Utopia.

The reality, however, is that you now get to hear what everyone got up to at the weekend. You get to enjoy tinny versions of other people's music from their earphones (or worse, their speakers). You hear every desk phone that rings, every text message that comes in, every vibrating phone, every tapping keyboard, every pair of heels walking around the office, every bad joke. Every time you look up you see other people's screens. Their work. Their *Facebook* pages. Their screen-savers. Their cats and children.

In small companies this can be inconvenient but scale it up and the large, modern agency is now so full of distractions that, for me at least, it became almost impossible to work efficiently in these spaces. Worse now than living in your office, you live within your screen. Not wanting to look away for fear of distraction. I never had an office. I arrived too late for that party but I really did miss it without ever experiencing it.

At least half of your job as a designer is to think. Perhaps I doth protest too much, but *Hemingway* didn't write whilst listening to other people's music.

Nor did *Da Vinci* sit three feet along a shared desk from someone eating their *Pret A Manger* sandwich or watching cat videos on *YouTube*. Your best thinking is done when it is quiet, when there are no distractions and when you are relaxed. When you remove those elements from the equation, the work immediately suffers.

Add to this mix the fact that many designers are often very shy about showing their work and are conscious that people don't see it before they're ready to share. For my part, most of my work looks very ugly before it looks any good. In an open environment, this is simply not tolerated and your work—unless you sit so close to your screen as to shield it from passers by—is on view to everyone who chooses to look. The problem being that self conscious designers don't take risks. They only put on their screen what they're sure will work, lest a Creative Director walk behind them and comment, unprovoked. A designer that doesn't take risks is one that should retire or be put down. Worse still is the idea that people can come and talk to you at any point. How many times must an idea be de-railed just as you're closing in on a solution to a brief when someone stops by for a chat? And now I sound old.

All
you
need
is
idea

The design course I attended didn't offer software training—as I understand is the case with many courses—and a former tutor of mine offered up some advice when we were approaching graduation. I may be paraphrasing here, but as I remember his words were:

"Never work for a company that asks you what software you can use at the interview."

His rationale was that they would just use you to churn out print-ready artwork and such. A *'Mac Monkey'* I believe was the term he used. Instead, our course focused much more on idea generation. There was less emphasis on polish and any learning of software was conducted in your own time.

That was ten years ago and now, having worked in situations where I've had a Junior Designer come in with no knowledge of software, I'm inclined to think that this was a pretty naïve statement to make, particularly to students looking for work. Although, with that said, I think it's now assumed that graduates will be familiar with at least the basics.

It's true that being able to think, problem solve and have ideas is (or should be) more than 50% of your role as a designer, but imagine turning up to your first day of work as a furniture maker with no knowledge of how to sand wood or use a chisel? The software you use is exactly that: a tool, and if you're unable to visualise your idea to a standard that the client will doubtless be expecting, then you'll very quickly find yourself out of work as there is precious little time for on-the-job training in industry. A company is perfectly within their rights to expect that you'll be able to come in, take a brief on day one and get to work that morning.

To that point, it could, and probably should be argued, that a Graphic Design course should offer training in at least the basic design software. To extend the analogy, who would enroll on a carpentry course and not expect to be taught how to use a chisel?

Ideas are important—really important—but so is having the means to bring them to life. Otherwise you're just an Art Director.

Joking. Sort of.

As *Thomas Edison* supposedly said, 'Vision without execution is hallucination'.

* * * * *

Nothing is original anymore

It's often said that 'everything has been done before' and I have so many problems with this statement that I barely know where to start.

The human brain is a wondrous and infinitely complex organ, its capabilities and limits still, as yet, undefined. When fed with the right combination of inspiration points a well educated, well read, hydrated and healthy brain will come up with original idea after original idea. As far as it is concerned.

And therein lies the rub.

Unfortunately (or fortunately, depending on your viewpoint) these days, a quick search online will reveal whether or not something has been executed before and to what extent but, put simply, it hasn't been executed by you. Your very involvement makes it an essentially original work and the desire to always be original can be an extremely stifling and creatively limiting way of working. It clouds your thinking and the pursuit of originality becomes an obsession that gets in the way of clear thought.

All you can do is try to come up with your best idea and realise it as well as you can. Far too much time is wasted thinking about other people's work. *Picasso* was a painter. He didn't invent painting, but he did do something new with it.

Equally, of course, the onus is on you as a designer to not seek to intentionally replicate someone's work and roll out the 'nothing is original' argument in your defence. Because that simply won't wash and you need to be honest with yourself. Let's face facts: no-one exists in a vacuum. You are and will continue to be inspired by other people's work. But, you are more than the sum of your parts and, hopefully, you will create new work that will go on to inspire others in turn.

* * * * *

People

care

about

design

Life has a tendency to put you in your place from time to time and I think something we all have to come to terms with is that, for the most part, the public really couldn't care less about what we do for a living.

Most people care about paying their bills. Getting their kids through school. Their health and their loved ones. Design, comparatively, is a distraction or a preoccupation. We're adrift; isolated from the lives of the majority. Design is perceived by most as a luxury. It's true that, when presented with something that is well designed, people will appreciate it but, given the choice, would your average consumer rather buy the £50 chair from their local furniture store or the £500 chair? Moreover, can your average consumer even afford the £500 chair over the £50 chair?

In part, the industry must shoulder some of the blame for the misconception that design is (or needs to be) expensive, exclusive and unnecessary. Frivolous, even.

You may very well turn up to the studio in ink-spattered jeans and a graphic print t-shirt but, to the majority—and I speak coming from a very working class background—design is synonymous with the black and white image of a well dressed, bespectacled man, sitting in an *Eames* chair in his white walled, loft-style apartment, surrounded by expensive lamps and *objets d'arts*. And it's an image that for a long time our industry has been happy to perpetuate. Look at the partner photographs on *Pentagram*'s website (or any of the large, old-school design firms for that matter), or most of the ads and features in *Wallpaper* or *Monocle*. That's what designers look like to the public. And it's not an image that the majority of people can identify with. They may be smiling—and we ourselves may know them to be good people—but there's something cold and stand-offish about it.

The problem is that this image is at odds with the reality. People don't think about [some kind of] a designer's hand being involved with everything—literally everything—that they come into contact with, be it a tin of beans or a family car. It's easy to point at expensive, luxury items and call them 'Designer Brands', but there's a real dignity in being the designer that makes a utility bill easier to understand for an elderly person. Or helping someone find their way through a crowded city centre or airport. This is the kind of design people interact with—and truly need—but don't really pay attention to or perhaps acknowledge as design. And that is sadly to be your lot in life.

And the really bad news? It's a lie that will continue to be told. We will continue to tell ourselves that people care about design, but it's not something that will change. Perhaps people do care about design but don't realise it. Perhaps they would care more if it were taken away. If road signs were suddenly hand painted, non-standardised and mis-spelt.

Half of the industry trades on the idea of producing desirable, luxury items (the fashion industry in particular has been running with this idea of design as an opulent, lifestyle-enriching purchase since time began), and that will be the public's continued broad perception of design. Blame *Lagerfeld*. Or *Coco Chanel*.

When you do worthwhile work, be happy with it. Know that you've made someone's life easier, communicated something more effectively or solved a problem. Just don't expect a standing ovation.

Print

is

dead

It's a rare occasion where I would take umbrage at the words of *Dr. Egon Spengler*. Without a word of a lie, I first heard the claim that 'print is dead' in the film *Ghostbusters*, released in 1984. The next time I even thought about it came with the publication of David Carson's book *The End of Print* in 1995. Even ten years after that, when we were riding the wave of the dot com boom and the tsunami-like ripples of its subsequent bust, still print played a major part in all of our lives.

Since then, however, a lot has happened. Today *Kodak* is bankrupt. Kodak! *Melody Maker* and *I.D Magazine* are long gone. In fact, over a thousand magazines have fallen out of print since 2008[1] (and taken with them scores of editorial designers who now struggle to find work) and the introduction of the *iPad* and e-book has tipped countless book stores, both large and small alike, into the pit of administration. Spengler's prophecy may yet come to fruition, albeit thirty years later.

And yet… Nobody appreciates the march of technology more than I, but the gung-ho attitude in which we've abandoned printed media of late—and with it over 4,000 years of human tradition—may eventually come back to bite us on the behind, unless you're willing to spend some serious cash.

[1] Source: gawker.com

I was recently introduced to the term 'bit rot'—the degradation of data over time. This is something I was hitherto unaware of and hadn't honestly considered, yet, it appears to be well documented and acknowledged by software and hardware manufacturers alike. The data we were told would never break, fade, crease or crack is apparently doing just that while it's sitting on your hard drive. Right now. In fact, several sources have been quoted as saying that if you want your grandchildren to see a specific image or photograph, then you should get a high quality print of it made that will last a lifetime. A statement that creaks and groans under the weight of its own irony.

Data has to live on something and 'something' always decays. Along with that comes the relentless rate of change in the way we store media. In my own lifetime I've watched *Betamax* and *VHS* cassettes become obsolete, audio cassettes, CD's, floppy disks, ZIP disks… a vast boneyard of defunct media exists out there somewhere. A manufacturer's warranty on a hard drive, for example, is a short three to five years, and constantly replacing these things is expensive. Really expensive for businesses whose main focus is data and data storage. On a smaller scale, imagine how many digital photos, e-books and MP3's you'll have amassed by the time you're ready to retire? With that said, they'll probably fit onto something smaller than the head of a pin by that point should *Moore's Law*[1] and *Raymond Kurzweil*[2] be believed.

With all this change, isn't there something comforting about the permanence of a book? Even if it only lasts 200 years, that's still many times longer than any other digital format has to date.

This is one, purely factual, reason that I believe print to be neither dead or dying. I thought I'd mention it first so as to appear emotionally detached from the subject, but that's really the crux of it: emotional engagement.

[1] *Moore's Law: that chip performance and the number of transistors on an integrated circuit doubles every 18 months.*
[2] *Raymond Kurzweil, author of* The Singularity is Near

You don't keep data in your wallet and show it to people. Data that makes you smile when you look at it, I mean. You don't cherish or frame or decorate your apartment walls with binary code, peering closely to observe the layers of ink and slight inaccuracies of the printing process that give it character and smell.

You don't—and can't—fondly leaf through e-books in the same way you would a printed book just for the sake of it—they don't enable you to engage with information in the same, freeform way—and, conversely, if you drop a book, it doesn't lose all its contents or need backing up anywhere. All this without mentioning the recent revelations that we don't actually own the songs and books that we have paid good money to download, merely we borrow them. The quandry of digital ownership will become a bigger issue in the coming years until existing policy is surely changed.

The design of books and magazines is too perfect; the engagement with print, too human. I agree that printed books can be cumbersome and e-books are true space savers in an increasingly crowded, space-starved world, that much is undeniable. Nor would I disagree with the fact that many of the magazines that have gone out of print need not have been published in the first place. In fact, the idea that there are several publications at any one time on cat breeds, hair styles, mobile phones and gardening is pretty absurd.

However, it was always my intention when writing this book that a printed version would exist, alongside an electronic version. Not out of (total) stubbornness or from being (entirely) old fashioned, but from a genuine desire for it to survive and be passed on.

Thank you for reading.

Postscript

There are a thousand or more authorities (of varying influence) on design and culture, each telling us what they believe to be this year's trend, this season's look, the next big thing and so on. All the way down to *'Designer of the Week'* features on some websites... Talk about making a commodity of a trade.

A former colleague of mine once told me about a Creative Director he had worked under who's catchphrase was "It's not a good idea until I say it's a good idea..." While I've never been unlucky enough to work under someone like that, it's vital to remember that ultimately, your opinion is as valid as anyone else's. It's your voice and individuality that will make your work original and relevant. If you find yourself creating work for other people, as opposed to yourself—that's to say, work that you know other people will like because it fits into a certain, well-defined mould—you betray yourself.

With all that said, no man or woman is an island. Completely shutting out the ideas and suggestions of others—whether they belong to a colleague, a client or a comment on your blog (though let's not kid ourselves, those anonymous social snipers making no constructive criticism should be treated with the contempt they deserve)—will eventually find you both literally and metaphorically adrift outside of industry. With larger, more commercial projects in particular, the more people you are designing for, the more opinions you should expect to present themselves. While one may relish the idea of being some cavalier, devil-may-care designer, blazing one's own trail over the horizon, the reality is that such an attitude is unworkable and it's important to acknowledge your audience and your clients' needs.

The English philosopher, logician and economist *John Stuart Mill* wrote that *"Popular opinions on subjects [not palpable to sense] are often true, but seldom or never the whole truth."* I couldn't agree more and hopefully one message above all others that you'll take away from this book is the importance of developing your own opinions about your work, your career and your working practices.

The subjects covered in this book weren't pulled from thin air, rather from conversations with peers, friends, colleagues and co-workers. Everyone, I found, has their own ideas with regards to the workings of the industry.

While I saw fit to put pen (fingers) to paper (keyboard) in this instance, I would never seek to project my own opinion on those who didn't ask for it and, while I believe there to be many popular lies about Graphic Design, I'd also be first to concede that there is rarely a singular truth.

About the author

Craig Ward is a British Designer and Art Director currently based in New York. Over the course of his career he has been lucky enough to work with some of the highest profile clients across the fashion, music, advertising and editorial fields.

A contributor to several industry journals, former *Art Directors' Club Young Gun* (2008), recipient of the *Type Director's Club 'Certificate of Typographic Excellence'* (2009) and *TEDx* speaker (2012), his work has been shown, awarded and documented globally in countless books, magazines and exhibitions.

He wanted to write a book. So he wrote a book. The alternative being to not write a book. Which would have been lazy.

http://www.wordsarepictures.com
http://www.twitter.com/mrcraigward

Photograph © *Steven Brahms*
Represented by Goldteeth & Co.

Contributors:

Sincere thanks to the following contributors whose involvement validated the project in my mind.

Brahms, Steven	*stevenbrahms.com*
Carson, David	*davidcarsondesign.com*
Cheuk, Deanne	*deannecheuk.com*
Clifford, Graham	*grahamclifforddesign.com*
Dean Dixon, Keetra	*fromkeetra.com*
Glaser, Milton	*miltonglaser.com*
Jung, Leo	*leojung.com*
Niemann, Christoph	*christophniemann.com*
Place, Michael, C.	*wearebuild.com*
Redman, Craig	*craigandkarl.com*
Rubino, Chris	*chrisrubino.com*
Sagmeister, Stefan	*sagmeister.com*
Sahre, Paul	*paulsahre.com*
Scott, Si	*siscottstudio.com*
Victore, James	*jamesvictore.com*
Ward, Craig	*wordsarepictures.com*
Wright, Ian	*mrianwright.co.uk*
Wong, Willy	*willywong.com*

References:

AIGA	*aiga.org*
Art Directors' Club	*adc.org*
D&AD	*dandad.org*
Goldteeth & Co.	*goldteethandco.com*
Kurzweil, Raymond	*kurzweilai.net*
Monocle	*monocle.com*
One Club, The	*oneclub.org*
Pentagram	*pentagram.com*
Rand, Paul	*paul-rand.com*
Saville, Peter	*petersaville.com*
Type Directors' Club	*tdc.org*
Vignelli, Massimo	*vignelli.com*
Wallpaper	*wallpaper.com*

Buy typefaces:

Commercial Type	*commercialtype.com*
House Industries	*houseind.com*
Höefler & Frere-Jones	*typography.com*
Hype For Type	*hypefortype.com*
Identikal	*identikal.com*
Linotype	*linotype.com*
Red Rooster	*houseoftype.com*
Virus Fonts	*virusfonts.com*

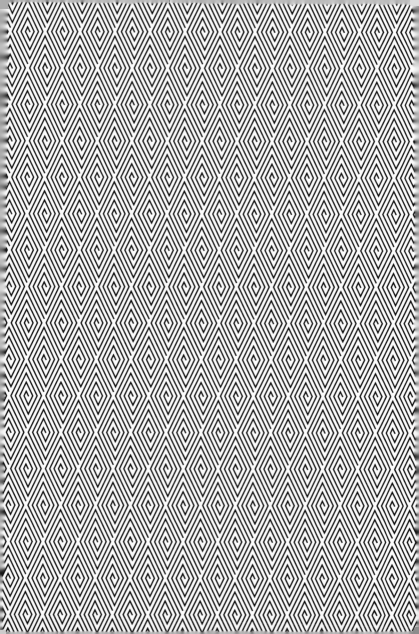